US ARMED FORCES

JOIN THE COAST GUARD

HOT TOPICS

By P. P. Mitchell

Gareth Stevens PUBLISHING

Please visit our website, www.garethstevens.com. For a free color catalog of all our high-quality books, call toll free 1-800-542-2595 or fax 1-877-542-2596.

Library of Congress Cataloging-in-Publication Data

Names: Mitchell, P. P., author.
Title: Join the Coast Guard / P. P. Mitchell.
Description: New York : Gareth Stevens Publishing, [2018] | Series: US Armed Forces | Includes index.
Identifiers: LCCN 2016059151| ISBN 9781538205389 (pbk. book) | ISBN 9781538205419 (6 pack) | ISBN 9781538205426 (library bound book)
Subjects: LCSH: United States. Coast Guard--Juvenile literature. | United States. Coast Guard--Vocational guidance--Juvenile literature.
Classification: LCC VG53 .M57 2018 | DDC 363.28/602373--dc23
LC record available at https://lccn.loc.gov/2016059151

Published in 2018 by
Gareth Stevens Publishing
111 East 14th Street, Suite 349
New York, NY 10003

Designer: Bethany Perl
Editor: Joan Stoltman

Photo credits: Cover, p. 1 (pilot) Justin Sullivan/Getty Images; cover, 1-32 (camouflage) 19srb81/Shutterstock.com; cover, pp. 1-32 (grunge effect) iulias/Shutterstock.com; cover, pp. 1-32 (rounded text box) foxie/Shutterstock.com; cover, pp. 1-31 (border) jumpingsack/Shutterstock.com; pp. 2-32 (text box) Olga_C/Shutterstock.com; pp. 5-29 (dog tag) Feng Yu/Shutterstock.com; photos courtesy of US Coast Guard: pp. 5, 7 by Petty Officer 3rd Class Ross Ruddell, p. 9 by Petty Officer 2nd Class Patrick Kelley, p. 11 by Petty Officer 3rd Class David Weydert, p. 13 assigned to NASA, p. 19 by U.S. Coast Guard photo, p. 23 by Petty Officer 2nd Class Cory J. Mendenhall, p. 25 by Petty Officer 1st Class Stephen Lehmann; p. 15 Tom Sperduto/U.S. Coast Guard via Getty Images; pp. 17, 29 (American Flag) Nataliia K/Shutterstock.com; pp. 21, 30 (service dress white uniform) MANDEL NGAN/AFP/Getty Images; p. 27 NASA/Mark H. Widick/Wikipedia.org; p. 29 Glynnis Jones/Shutterstock.com; p. 30 (service dress blue uniform) Paul Morigi/WireImage/Getty Images; p. 30 (undress uniform) Desiree Navarro/WireImage/Getty Images.

Printed in the United States of America

CPSIA compliance information: Batch #CS17GS: For further information contact Gareth Stevens, New York, New York at 1-800-542-2595.

CONTENTS

INTRODUCING THE COAST GUARD

The coast guard is the smallest US military force, but it's given many **missions**. As a coastguardsman, you'll always be busy! Our country has thousands of miles of coast that the coast guard keeps safe every day.

DID YOU KNOW?

Even though everyone in the US Coast Guard is called a coastguardsman, all jobs are open to women. Women lighthouse keepers in the 1800s were the first female guardsmen, though they weren't given titles or trained.

From guarding waters and coastlines from pollution to carrying out **rescues** at sea, coastguardsmen have many important jobs to do. Coastguardsmen also break through ocean ice so boats can travel north. They even stop illegal drugs from coming into our country!

DID YOU KNOW?

The president has the power to call the coast guard off their regular duties and into battle as part of the US Navy.

6030
CAPE COD
U.S.
COAST GUA D
RESCUE
USCG

WHAT DOES A COASTGUARDSMAN DO?

Based on your skills, what you like, and what jobs are open, there are many career paths you might take within the coast guard! You could do maintenance, or fix things, on a **cutter**, or work with maps and guiding, **engineering**, radio, or even **welding**.

DID YOU KNOW?

Most coastguardsmen have training in law enforcement, or making people obey laws. **Environmental** laws, safety laws, international laws, and many other laws are all a part of the coast guard's mission.

Coastguardsmen can be trained to carry out medical tasks in emergency situations, such as when they are rescuing someone. They can be lighthouse operators or in charge of making sure boats have enough supplies before setting sail.

DID YOU KNOW?

In 2012 alone, the Coast Guard had almost 20,000 search-and-rescue missions and 3,000 pollution missions and saved over 4,000 lives!

ENLISTING

One way to join the coast guard is to enlist after high school. A recruiter is the person in your community you'll talk to about enlisting after you've decided what branch of the armed forces you'd like to join.

DID YOU KNOW?

"Enlisting" means "choosing to join the military." As an enlisted coastguardsman, your days will include serving on missions by completing your orders.

UNITED STATES
COAST GUARD
LASHANDA HOLMES
LT
USCG

After meeting with the recruiter, you'll take a test. That will help the coast guard see your natural skills and talents so they can match you to the right job. Then you'll need to pass an exercise test.

DID YOU KNOW?

Basic training, the last step before you're officially a guardsman, is 8 weeks of workouts, swimming drills, and classes in first aid, weapons, and more.

U.S. COAST GUARD
MASON
U.S. COAST GUARD

BECOMING AN OFFICER

Officers plan missions and give enlisted coastguardsmen their orders. Your decisions are important and may even mean life or death at times. Officers have 4-year college degrees and special training to handle the responsibility and leadership of their job.

COAST GUARD RANKS

OFFICERS

COMMANDANT OF THE COAST GUARD, ADMIRAL CHIEF OF NAVAL OPS

VICE ADMIRAL

REAR ADMIRAL

CAPTAIN

COMMANDER

ENLISTED

MASTER CHIEF PETTY OFFICER OF THE COAST GUARD

COMMAND MASTER CHIEF PETTY OFFICER

MASTER CHIEF PETTY OFFICER

SENIOR CHIEF PETTY OFFICER

CHIEF PETTY OFFICER

DID YOU KNOW?

The higher the rank in any armed force, the more pay, responsibility, and skill that person has earned. Enlisted coastguardsmen and officers are ranked separately.

There are several ways to become an officer. You can join the College Student Pre-Commissioning Initiative (CSPI) as a college sophomore and train during school. After graduation, you would then go to the 17-week Officer Candidate School (OCS).

DID YOU KNOW?

In OCS, you'll do lots of physical training and take courses in leadership, ship operation and maintenance, **navigation**, and more.

U.S. COAST GUARD

You could go to the US Coast Guard Academy (USCGA) in New London, Connecticut, for college. It's hard to get into—only about 250 freshman spots are available! You would major in engineering, government, management, environmental science, or marine science.

DID YOU KNOW?

Most USCGA students will continue on to graduate school after getting their degree.

BARRS
U.S. COAST GUARD

You can also become an officer by getting a 4-year degree without being in CSPI and then applying to OCS. Or you may graduate with a degree in law, medicine, flight, or engineering, and then apply to be an officer through direct commission, or order.

DID YOU KNOW?

Direct commission training is in New London, Connecticut. Enlisted coastguardsmen can also apply for this program if they want to rise in the ranks to become an officer.

HELICOPTER RESCUE SWIMMERS

Only a few guardsmen have passed the training to earn the title of rescue swimmer. These heroes jump out of helicopters into scary situations and pull people out of the water, saving their lives! They're strong and brave—and really good swimmers!

DID YOU KNOW?

Everyone in the coast guard must be able to dive from a block and swim 100 meters (109 yards) in 5 minutes without goggles and without touching the sides of the pool. They also have to be able to tread water for 5 minutes with no safety vest.

COASTGUARDSMAN IN SPACE?

Coast guard divers were called in for the National Aeronautics and Space Administration (NASA) NEEMO 16 mission. The underwater mission trained astronauts for space. They needed the coastguardsmen to do underwater construction and navigation.

DID YOU KNOW?

There have been two coast guard astronauts! Commander Bruce Melnick had 5,000 hours of flight time as a coastguardsman before flying for NASA. Captain Daniel Burbank was an astronaut for nearly 2 decades!

HOW CAN I GET READY NOW?

To get ready for the coast guard, you'll need good grades in math and science classes. Keep your body in shape by playing sports or exercising. The coast guard is a great way to proudly guard and serve our country.

UNITED STATES COAST GUARD ETHOS

I AM A COAST GUARDSMAN.
I SERVE THE PEOPLE OF THE UNITED STATES.
I WILL PROTECT THEM.
I WILL DEFEND THEM.
I WILL SAVE THEM.
I AM THEIR SHIELD.
FOR THEM I AM SEMPER PARATUS.*
I LIVE THE COAST GUARD CORE VALUES.
I AM PROUD TO BE A COAST GUARDSMAN.
WE ARE THE UNITED STATES COAST GUARD.

*"SEMPER PARATUS" IS LATIN FOR "ALWAYS READY" AND IS THE COAST GUARD'S SAYING.

DID YOU KNOW?

Part of basic training includes learning the words of the Coast Guard Ethos by heart. You can start preparing early by learning it now!

COAST GUARD UNIFORMS

SERVICE DRESS WHITE UNIFORM

SERVICE DRESS BLUE UNIFORM

UNDRESS UNIFORM

FOR MORE INFORMATION

Books

Gordon, Nick. *Coast Guard Rescue Swimmer*. Minneapolis, MN: Bellwether Media, 2013.

Markovics, Joyce L. *Today's Coast Guard Heroes*. New York, NY: Bearport Publishing, 2012.

Orr, Tamra B. *Your Career in the Coast Guard*. New York, NY: Rosen Publishing, 2012.

Websites

Learn About the United States Coast Guard

uscg.mil/community/coloringbook/index.html#/1/

Print, color, and read this coloring book packed with facts about the US Coast Guard on every page.

U.S. Coast Guard Museum Collection

uscg.mil/hq/cg092/museum/museumcollections.asp

Take an online tour of many of this museum's cool pieces of coast guard history.

Publisher's note to educators and parents: Our editors have carefully reviewed these websites to ensure that they are suitable for students. Many websites change frequently, however, and we cannot guarantee that a site's future contents will continue to meet our high standards of quality and educational value. Be advised that students should be closely supervised whenever they access the Internet.

GLOSSARY

cutter: any ship over 65 feet (20 m) in length

engineering: the use of science and math to build better objects

environmental: having to do with the world around us

mission: a task or job a group must perform

navigation: the science of plotting and following a path from one place to another

rescue: to free a person or thing from unsafe conditions

weld: to join metal parts together by heating

INDEX